Composte:
Recycling Freedom Through Language

Jerome White

Copyright © 2007 by Jerome White

All Rights Reserved

ISBN

978-0-6151-6032-0

Acknowledgments

I would like to once again thank everyone who has helped me arrive at a place in life where I could pen these words, including Joseph Faulkner and Dr. Kerry Hofheimer. Still, to all my teachers, I owe you a debt that I can never repay. You were true inspirations that kindled that fire inside me to devour knowledge, write and not take either for granted. There is a little of each one of you in every word I scratch on the page. You pushed, pulled, and guided me along my path and for that, I am truly grateful.

Dedication

For my teachers & my family

Composte:

Recycling Freedom Through Language

"Man is condemned to be free; because once thrown into the world, he is responsible for everything he does."
Jean-Paul Sartre

An Old Flame

*When you have a fire
burning inside you,
you don't put it out
when you scratch it on a page,
smear it against the canvas,
or scribble it down
on staff after staff,
no.
You open it up
and fan those flames
harder and faster
so that all who will see
can understand
and be warmed by the same
fire that burns inside you.*

Table of Contents:

Introduction   14

Happiness   18
- *Family*   20
- *What A Life*   22
- *Prismatic Light*   24
- *Almost A Frost*   26
- *Mountain Morning*   28
- *ODU Café*   30
- *America's Times Past*   32
- *Rain*   34
- *Star Dust*   36
- *The Tye River*   38

Life & Death   40
- *One more Night*   42
- *On The Road*   44
- *Growing Older**   48
- *Growing Younger**   49
- *The Death of a Leaf*   50
- *Your Future*   52

Love   54
- *Bounce Back*   56
- *Perfect Together*   58
- *The Thought Of...*   60

Inquiry   62
- *Redeemer*   64
- *Wait*   66
- *Sleepy Splinters*   68
- *Awakened*   70
- *Lost*   72

- Regrets	76
- The Death of an Artist	78
- While Writing A Poem In America	80
- Capital Storm	82
- We Are Inhibiting Ourselves	84
- Fear of Freedom	86

God   90

- *God's Breath*   92
- *God's Snakes*   94
- *Sweet & Sour*   96
- *Middle Ground*   98
- *In the Name of Knowledge*   100

History   102

- *A Night with Bruno*   104
- *Lost and Found*   110

Introduction

Texts are one of the few sources that exist which allow us to truly trace or detect history. These collections of thoughts and ideas represented in the symbolic order only by words scratched or printed on a page give a sense of what it was like to live in the past. They provide readers with a map that traces the birth and path of various ideas. One such concept is the idea of freedom. We cannot only follow the path of freedom itself through the use of texts, but we can also logically detect the rise and need for such a concept in language in the first place. Early humans, controlled by no others but them selves were innately free to make the choices about how they read or interpreted and acted in the world around them. For those individuals, there would have been no need for a word to convey an idea that did not exist yet. In the small pre-stratified societal structures that those early "speaking" humans functioned within, the nature of the wild was the only reality they knew. However, as soon as one human enacted his or her rule, or view of the world over others, then there was born the idea of control or domination which inevitably was symbolically expressed through language. This split basic thought into two separate categories: concepts freely created through independent interpretation of the world and concepts that were preordained by someone else who chose to force his or her view of the world on an oblivious group of people. Subsequently, dichotomy between individuals who freely interpreted the world around them and those who either from fear or by force saw the world through "preordained" eyes was born, or the grand dichotomy in its infancy: the self versus the world. When freedom was born, necessarily, slaves were also born.

Freedom is a concept that has been argued over, fought for, and consequently written about for centuries. Throughout the world, literature has been created about this topic for every imaginable audience and for every imaginable motive and reason. Many of those in power, the power being of a state or some type of court, have argued against those inherent properties of freedom that allow individuals to interpret the world for themselves and thus, freely act on those interpretations, for everyone except themselves, because of some inherent right to rule they argue that only they possess. Some explained the world as being created and maintained by use of the hierarchical systems that preserved their rule and equally stifled the freedom of those that worked to provide them with a people or country to rule over in the first place. Freedom has also been argued away by those rulers through the use of religious doctrine found in texts that were, for the most part, written or interpreted by them. These texts, in many cases, were supposedly, "received directly" from God by those in power who alone had the "freedom" to read and interpret those texts. Subsequently, their reading of the religious and secular texts and thus the world itself became an absolute that all must adhere to, even eventually the rulers themselves. However, they did have the right to change their reading at any time when it came in direct conflict with current problems associated with maintaining their rule.

The ruled, on the other hand, have always discussed freedom and the inherent properties of that freedom. Freewill for every individual can be read in these same religious texts and the world itself, according to the ruled, given free reign to do so. Interpretation so becomes an issue inherent in the notion of freedom. We as humans do naturally "see and/or read" things from different perspectives. So according to the ruled, and even some rulers who were or had been ruled themselves, there was a need for a discussion about freedom in order to not only attain it, but also preserve it. We can reenter this discussion by seeing the many texts that it helped create.

Literature itself, given its inherent properties of the reader's freedom to read, has changed dramatically over time. From the strict formal verse of the poetry dictated by those to some extent in power, to the free form verse and multi-perspective and novelistic features of some modern literary forms, language itself, historically read by us through literature, and freedom are forever linked. Literature, or merely the written word, is the forum through which it is argued and defined. Language created the need for freedom, and it is language that many have believed will be the solution to the dilemma for the need for such a notion in the first place.

Happiness

Family

They're like a cozy old coat
that fits just snugly enough
to warm you in a close and comforting way,
there wrapped around you
down in the very depths of frigid despair,
when everything and everyone else
has faded far from sight,
lifting you, raising your hopes up
to feel the heat of their light
warming your face once again.

They know what you want
before you even ask for it
and keep life happy
by sharing more than just your name,
but who you are, were, and one day will become,
a connection to your past
that allows you to feel a wholeness with time,
a completeness and cycle that disappears
in their absence like
the color fades from the flower's face
as summer gives way to fall.

Hold them close
and remember
while you snugly squeeze and listen softly
to savor every moment of their sweet embrace,
every sound in every echoing voice,
every small detail.
For all good things,
especially those that you love and need the most,

no matter how strong or secure they seem
always suddenly get snatched away
when least expected.

So, teach them to know and remember
how to be the glue
that holds all your pieces of life tightly together,
to fit firmly
so they can remain strong enough
to bear the weight of those who have yet to come,
and snugly enough to hold together the home
that keeps the fires burning
for every child that becomes lost
out in the cold.

What a Life

Wake up;
smell that rich strong coffee
and the sweet aroma the flowers make
like candy boiling in grandma's kitchen.

Feel the warmth of the sun
just peeking through the windows
scraping off that bedtime chill
from the night before.
Can you hear those cute little melodies
rise and fall with the anticipation
of their first squirmy meal of the day?

With a cup of black,
then laid outside
see the sun wisp through
those sharp blades of grass
like a thousand lights
through a jagged house of mirrors.

What a life:

The air,
cleaner than that smell
just after stepping out of the shower.

The sky,
it's not really blue
but appears bluer
than the clearest
ocean looks like from afar.

Now see the trees
as they stretch in the wind
as if they wanted
the exercise,
everything in its place,
doing what it should.

Now drink, smell, feel,
hear, and see the perfection of life.

It's there.

Prismatic Light

A different and fresh day has dawned
as bright and fiery
as any reclaimed soul
risen from the ashes in the very depths
of hell.
The newness of this prismatic light
paints all things that had been greyed
with a dripping richness
that warms and washes the eyes.

These new colors ignite the imagination
once again.

The split of those reds,
coursing through all the pedals
of the roses pumping and
exciting the mind
to passionate flights of hope,
burns deep and bright
into the once cold core
of the slumbering heart.

And those shafts of yellow
just splintering there around each soft pedal
of the gentle sunflower,
dance in the morning heat,
caressing and calming the sensing soul
ready to accept the world
with a new and wondrous sense of zeal.

Oh, and that orange glow
hovering over every center
of each now opened daffodil,

paints the world
and waxes the wit,
heating up those empirical p-arts of the mind
that have been waiting,
wanting to awaken.

And ahhh the blues,
those calming balming blues
rolling soft and steadily
down each violet's blossom
cooling and soothing the soul
with their homespun shades
and many layered veins
that pulse
to the very beat of the world.

And every green that grows
and breathes full the lungs of life,
now beams
with an earthly cadence of light
that allows the world to know its there,
allows the mind, the body,
and every space in-between
to know their place (in line,
in time).

The day has come.
Awaken to the life
given freely.
Drink in all that flows from this
newly discovered and fleeting dawn.

Almost A Frost

The dew is but two degrees
from crystal
and hesitant to turn to vapor
even in the brightness
of the new morning heat.

While the twinkle of the sun
just peeks between
the weather worn slats
of the fence,
the tiny blades of grass
bounce back and forth
like the needles of a Richter scale
as the wind blows ever so slightly
across the backyard.

It's now cold enough
for the first time this year
to see my outward breath
press the air in front of me
like the steam
firing from the lid of
an early morning pressure cooker.

Slowly, the sun illuminates
the nearly frozen trees
only to thaw them enough
to sway
in a meek unison
with the now almost weighty wind.

The pine needles
that haven't turned brown

and fallen yet, glisten
in the brightness of our star.
They look as if
they're almost frozen
and act as, long,
thin prickly prisms.

Mountain Morning

Remember those days that smiled
    upon our heads
    with the warmth
    of a smooth June sunrise,
    when you, there beautifully sleeping
    awoke?

Snuggled safe together on the bed,
    you felt like a soft warm glow
    surrounding me like the heat of a fire
    that fills every spot in my body
    on a cold Blue Ridge night.

Your sleeping head,
    there resting upon my shoulder
    where God created that pillow
    just for you,
    was perfect.

Remember when your eyes lifted,
    and you saw me there
    gazing upon you, wishing
    that time didn't exist.

Then, as our heads and hearts
    again grew closer,
    meeting in a fourth of July
    extravaganza with the embrace
    of our early morning kiss,
    our eyes danced.

The sound we made as our faces met
    and our kiss was consummated

      echoed through the valley
      falling forever upon that wild river
      to be heard bouncing down the rocks
      until one day drowning in an endless ocean
      of dreams.

Every time I hear the running of rushing water,
      I can see those seeing twins dancing
      in the light of our summer star,
      opening a day in a new world
      freshly discovered every morning
      I awaken next to you.

There, you are gladly emblazoned
      onto my eyes and heart
      as I am
      on yours.

ODU CAFE

Backwards, OPEN, neon pink and
Outside, big yellow cheeze bus buzzes by
while Black Rich Bean, perfumes the air thick.
Bic-flick; winston, inhaled
over velvet green floor.
Walnut stained grained on the wall
A framed memory, A KISS-
That black and white dog wants to leave
Fire rays pierce the eye through glass
    I'm hit!
A corner of confusion
A black or whitey-yellow head
Awake or Numbed?

Waiter; tray rattles, glass shop
People's static all around as-
Blue guitar drips fifths of sound
From the black round cones.
Pour, splash, drip; another glass filled
Sax screams in pain, Bronze
A Conversation: video; tapes games, adolescence.

Table, glass on mesh sack top;
Smash, fire gone; butt
Clear square fills up with ash.
Outside, horn screamed, tire squeals squeaky.
Open door nothing new
Sit down, Shut up, order.
Sizzle splat, meat on a grill-
They'll have a burger-
A finger in the air; "Hey"
Empty: another please; whispered

"Sure", reassured

Motion, silhouetted cars and
A black and white flat drama-
      busily bouncing by,
The dog, the kiss; he still wants to go.

America's Times Past

Brown, dust blown
miniature cyclones
with rust, fading
in and out.

Hot dog smells
breezing over on the wind
and yells,
where the chili
had already hit.

Crack- the ball
in the air
slow moe,
a double denied.

Hey batter batter chatter
rises through the bug
busy traffic
of the field, and

Fresh cut green blades
aroma with-dandelion
buttercup glow.

A pitch, a swing:
white round with red thread
not hitting the ground
until it's
too late.

Glaring stare
at the hitter of the homer;
that pitcher's pissed.

Rain

Dry brown
yellow grass on the ground
with only a slight
sliver of green is

Seen by all
who thirst
for one quenching
drip of life.

Blue sky with
puffy cotton
growing perfect
on its vast open fields
but then,

Darkness creeps in,
the sky goes away
and all that
fluffy candy with it.

A white light splits
through the air
a crack, a tree;
fire sparks.

Now, bowls
of water
separately tossed
through a great fan
smack the dry life.

Below, rivers form

from the ground
denying entry
at first
but then,

The thirst is quenched, and
all gets sucked up
like spilt coffee
on a dry, dry sponge
gone in an imaginary
minute.

Wet, damp leaves sag
and wait
for their bellies to be
filled once again
by life.

Star Dust

Wrestle with the sunlight,
  coerce it
  and then tie it in a bow
so that it drips dreams of wonder
  into a warm pool
  that glistens as it glows.

Bathe in its brilliance;
  cup your hands
  and drink in the light.
Feel the warmth then ooze from your body
  as your day peels away
  to night.

See your star blaze
  mirrored from within,
  tasting it as
  it washes between your lips.
This growing twinkle
  that is now within you
  will flow freely
  as you blow a kiss

to the Heavans that hover
  above, below, and besides;
For all the stars that breathe life
  and share the journey,
  it is in us
  that they subside.

The Tye River

White bubbles foam up
  and rush by rapidly
  as a dusty dry piece of gray
  peeks up through the madness
Surrounded by wet,
  this stone stands its ground well,
  for now.

A yellow five pointed star
  falls from the sky
  hitting its smooth gray brother,
  and then the wind
  wisps it into the drink.
There it goes
  steadily bouncing
  down its bumpy path.

A shower of dried red blossoms
  slowly drifting down then
  floats on a broken sheet of glass;
  ever on they go.
Soon they will reach
  their slowing destination
  where all motion stops
  in a deep blue dream.

Long round hollow ghosts
  of days gone by
  drape over the flowing gap
  like bridges spanning time.
Bird nests like dried clumps of grass
  sit on these trestles
  with tenants awaiting their first
  squirmy meal of the day;

perhaps it will float by
                          or maybe not.

Life & Death

Life & Death

One More Night

Torn, tight and sore
are your muscles
as you stretch your tired arms towards the sky
with a huge vocal yawn: 'yyaahhhh.'

Your eyelids grow heavy
with the weights
of the long day gone by,
slowly pulling shut your
crystal view on the world.

As your sight begins to blur
and everything,
everything
comes in and out of focus
waving at you like the surface of
a humid street on a hot summer day,

your rest, inevitable, is welcomed,
wanted
to refresh your heavy tired eyes
for their next day,
a new fresh and bright hopeful vision of life.

Each night as the darkness of sleep
creeps upon you,
you face that slice of time with
an almost eerie reluctance,
even though without this
recess from conscious existence,
life could not go on.

But, with no worries
and with new chances,

you embrace the
temporary darkness
of sleep.

Still, what
when the light of the world blurs
swaying from within and outside of time,
when your eyes
flicker like a small candle in
a stiff breeze,
when all life begins to fade like
another day,
another rainbow dissolving
in the billowing
of the dark clouds of a thickening storm,
as you feel breathless,
something pressing on your chest
squeezing the air from your body,
draining the brightness of life from your eyes,
with the darkness chasing you
for the last time?

Have you done everything
you needed or wanted to today?
Did you tell them how much they mattered,
how much you always cared,
how thankful you were for eveything
and how sorry you were?

Is it different,
or simply one more night of
acceptance?

ON THE ROAD

My whole life,
I've been racing down a titanic highway,
a wild interstate
filled with too many exits.

Occassionally, I'd slow down for a while
and take one of those ready ramps,
rumble off the highway
and see what there was to see
and do what there was to do.

But always,
I returned,
returned to the road
rolling along in the same direction
with a careful abandonment.

Sometimes I'd fly,
no limits or laws,
but there were always
those rest stops where
I could idle for a while,
take a brake and think.

Each time though, the roar
fell again on my ears
pulling back,
pulling the door shut
and my foot to the floor.

> However,
> I've run this race for far too long
> and now have reached the end
> of this long many laned bi-way.

Ahead, there is but one way now,
one small lane that
rambles slowly
onward into the wooded expanse
and unsure distance.

I have to carefully choose right now
for the first time
since I put pedal to floor.

Do I go forward
on this dusty drive,
brake-check
and experience the sites
unknown to me
but for secondhand
neon signs.

Or, should I turn around,
roll and go back the way I came,
find one of those
many frivolous exits
and bury myself in the hasty ways
of what was.

What do I do,
Keep going a little frightened
and unsure
but with a safe and grounded
sense of right?
Or, do I turn around and hope
for a contented exit
that leads to a contented town?

Hum?

I guess I'll go.
I 'll move on
off the highway
into the small expanse
of a narrative like race
that has finished its beginning.
For even though the flags are crossed
and the middle has just begun,
the checkered ending is definitely on its way, safely.
But that's okay.
All good trips like good tales
must reach some conclusion
to make way for the new ones,
the spin-offs that always occur
on the road.

Growing Older

I wanna grow up
I wanna be older
I wanna be big
I wanna be bolder

I wish I could see
I wish I could drive
I wish I knew how
  Things come alive

      That's what I want now
      And I don't care how
      I want tomorrow to come
      I want today to be done

I wanna grow up
I wanna be older
I wanna be big
I wanna be bolder

Growing Younger

I need to go back
I need to go home
I need to return
I need not to roam

I wish I could still see
I wish I could still drive
I wish I knew how
  Things stay alive

      That's what I want then
      A new chance to begin
      I need yesterday to come
      I need today to be done

I need to go back
I need to go home
I need to return
I need not to roam

The Death of a Leaf

Pale splotches of brown
surround an almost vacant
reminiscence of green.

There, the stem,
a bent stick pushing its way
past the dead torn veins
of days gone by
when a shade of chlorophyll
wrapped itself around life,
is weakened.

But now, ripped edges
sit covered in a civilization
of red six legged torrid soldiers
sucking the last grain of green
from this ovular shaped corpse.

Underneath this drained member
that once belonged to a greater whole
sits chaos;
yellow green pointy strands
of natural silken skin
now mock the dead.

A clover for luck,
now prays
just beside this crypt,
hoping that it won't be
the next seasonal victim
of change.

Your Future

Rabid flies
swarm like bees
searching
for the last red flower
on earth

While pale green skeletons
lie rancid
in their own
petrified remains.

Now, the water is gone,
absorbed
by all the dead reeking fish
afloat on a dry sea
like sponges.

This morning, the ghosts of birds
rose through the air
on the stench of a world
rotting,
only to be burned
by that infectious
hovering inferno
ever growing and
consuming the wind.

And there,
the people sit
in their domes
smiling.

53

Love

Bounce Back

Wishing your smile was here
to brighten the flowers
and make their pale colors more than yellow
in the soft unbending pedals of the sunflowers,
extra fiery red in the many layered blossoms of the zinias
and still, even more gently green
on all the varied foliage of the garden,
I wait.

The Light, slanted and bouncing
off the rippling water of the pond
rhythmically moves
with the widening rings
as they reach the edge
and slightly bounce back.

As I linger here and watch,
I can see the reciprocal nature of life.
Seasons come
with setting of the sun
but cyclically they return.
Colors fade and branches sag,
and still they once again fill themselves
with all the vibrant color of life.

As the wind slowly bends the trees
swaying back and forth
with their leaves singing
with the choral hiss of creation,
there again is a rhythm,
a metronome to living.

The child's ball bounces.
It's thrown down, but always springs back

behind the weather worn
slats of the fence in strobe effect
as he hurriedly runs by to catch up.

I believe and bide the in-between times,
those that fit
sometimes not so neatly
between the night and day.
The Twilight, although confusing
and often frightening
always gives way to the rising of a new dawn.

But without the night,
without the picturesque drooping of the flowers,
and the frigid barren emptiness of the winters,
we could never again feel
the eastern spring sunrise of new beginnings.

So, as the water gently
grows in time across the width of the pond,
I await the bouncing back
of the soft wet ripples
as they meet themselves
once again in the middle.

Perfect Together

Steaming golden chunks of moist apples,
  the swelling aroma of cinnamon in the air,
  and that light flaky crust.
Vanilla bean dots in a freezing white scoop
  of flavored snow, melting,
  dripping down over that scrumptious triangle of pie.

      Wonderful apart yet,
      perfect together.

Skin like, silken scarlet petals round and smooth as night
  budding from a simple light shiny green stem
  covered with razor sharp sacred needles, cut.
Spirited green hairs bouncing in the breeze
  topped with the purity of white baby blossoms
  against the strength of that majestic red bloom.

      Beautiful apart yet,
      complete together.

Billowy white mist, puffy as cotton
  sculpted into great hovering creatures of the air
  floating ever so softly across the sky, at the pace of tiny
  snails.
Huge majestic green covered giants stand etched by a master
  stretching beautiful wooded lands from the sea to the roof of
  the world,
  with such slight halos of pure white water vapor covering
  their peaks.

      Mighty apart yet,
      heavenly together.

Friendly black satin darkness stretches across the space of
 night
  ever there to calm and soothe the soul
  with an emptiness that is full of life.
There, twinkling little friends of the night light our ways
  illuminating our lives by the fire of ancient times
  showing where we've been and perhaps where we will one
  day be.

    Two different things,
    two different people
    brilliant apart yet,
    perfect together.

The Thought Of...

never seeing your sweet little smile,
or feeling your soft beautiful legs
rub against mine while,
you roll over with your rosy cheeks
and bright green/grey eyes
opening for the first time
of each day as you yawn and say
"Good morning baby,"

not hearing your laugh
as you chuckle at anything that strikes you,
whether it be Gidgette, me,
or something you heard
FES say on TV,

not ever picking you up off the ground
and swinging you round and around
then gently setting you back down to the floor
and softly patting your sweet little bottom
once more,

never watching as you quiet
and softly sleep
and wait for our next day
when we once again meet
as for the first time,
us thinking your thoughts and mine,

not ever seeing you enjoy
me cooking dinner for you
as a child would a toy
and seeing in your eyes the smile
that wants to love with me a while,

never sweetly pressing our faces together
in a long loving kiss filled forever
with all that we have for and in each other, tasting your lips
as we softly become one and kiss,
hearing that little smack at the end of our touch
as you smile, and we think at the exact same time,
"I Love You So Much..."

is too much to bear.

Inquiry

Redeemer

Can redemption,
        a salve there to soothe and cool
        the burning wounds left open by indecision
        like a rope thrown to someone falling,
        reaching for hope,
        gasping for some small hint of air
        found but in a true and guilt free life,
only be given or received by means of the evil
one abides or a sin someone else commits?

Is redemption
        A lie stretched back
        to the beginning of time,
        there to help pass
        the complying days of life calmly
        that still invariably lead to an unknown
        and unexpected doom,
taken only by those who feel life
can no longer be endured without it,
or end satisfactorily, let alone at all,
in its absence?

Can redemption,
        A gift that warms the mind
        like kind words on a cold day
        served with steam creamed sugar and coffee
        given to one in desperate need
        of some kind of enlightening answer
        to the plaguing and weighty question of why,
be asked for or sought after to mend the tears of a life wasted,
one not lived in earnest to its pure potential?

Does redemption,

        a light that shows the way
        on thick cloudy nights
        where direction is relative
        and no way and every way seem right,
give meaning, a map which leads us
on our way to a life that is full of all the riches
both in pleasure and pain, to give this new life
to someone who has lost his own?

WAIT

Will there ever be another morning
   when you can go outside and inhale life
   and then give it back to everything
   with each puff of air that gently pulses
   from your mouth?

Will ever there be another noon
   when you can drink some water;
   water that is so pure and clean
   that it refreshes you enough to want to live
   and cool and clear enough
   to gently make the sun and you
   need each other?

Will ever the evening come again
   when you look forward to the earth
   shedding off its light coat of day
   so that that picturesque picture
   of those twinkling children of the night
   bring to your eyes
   with a brilliance that seems to last forever
   a feeling of awe?

Will the midnight ever come again
   when you dream of the love
   of the world that brings life to all,
   of things that make the stars come to you
   like friends with the gift of light,
   of things that make sleeping and waking hours
   mirror images of joy?

And, will you ever look forward again
   to that beautiful flower named sun

coming over the green wooded hills
breaking through the darkness, giving life
just peeking through the trees
grazing your face ever so slightly
like a mother feeling the head of her child?

Wait for a day when the warm redness
  of the eastern dawn will wash away
  all the bloody hate of a world
  that has turned against itself.
  Wait; it might come?

Sleepy Splinters

Today, my heart got
pounded and split apart
by a deceptive meat clever.
Parts splattered insane
all over the walls
of my mind,
ripped up, out of order and
lost,
were spread like dirty,
rotten-raspberry-butter-jam
all over my floor.

      Then, clumsily
      as I tried in vain
      to piece back together
      what little fragments remained,
      an invisibly wicked vice tightened slowly
      and squeezed the segments
      of something recently lost
      back together,
      dripping drop by drop,
      staining the ground
      by leaving a impassioned red Pollack painting
      wherever I passed.

Wanting relentlessly, I ran
while once remembered thoughts
ripped through my mucked up mind
like tiny atomic explosions
emitted exponentially
in the center of some great glass lake
inside my intranquil head.
I suffered the splinters of a shattered silence

rippling and stitching shut my ears,
blocking all the soothing sounds
there to salve the open sores
of passion worn on the inside
of my once unblemished soul.

    Still, adamantly
    I tried...
    Tried in vain to hear the faint whispers
    of hope flow through my body,
    but my mangled mind grew painfully numb
    needling me
    so out of touch
    with the sensibilities
    of undying hope
    that now, I sit emotionally
    motionless and,

    Only one thing
    can sew my heart
    back together
    stitch by stitch
    and can keep it beating
    in time with the love
    once in me. This one thing alone
    can choose to be the pill to my pain.
    But this pill is filled with all the needles
    that prick at my hand as it sleeps,
    and I can't swallow it.

Awakened

I lived in a dream,
  crimson cream filled
  with daffodils, and
  rose pedals
  where fresh bread baked,
  always rising
  straight from the oven,
  filling the whole house
  with the warm and welcoming smells
  of family.

I lived in a dream,
  heart pounding
  soul mate sounding
  in a perfect time that played
  the sweet rhythms of love
  over and over again singing
  all the sweet sowing sing songs
  of a perfect harmonious world.

I lived in a dream,
  slumbering softly
  upon river side highlands,
  listening to the hissing wind
  and the lofty trees
  talk for hours
  about what I was thinking.

I lived in a dream,
  never stirring
  to see the others
  that cared for and shared me
  with all the wonder of perfection,
  the only way it comes.

I lived in a dream
unfortunately, I woke up.

Lost

When everything
that I count on
like the stars dotted light
in the night sky
and the continual rotation of the earth
bringing forth the new day
suddenly goes away,
I'm confused.

As my whole world:
past, present, and future,
hopes and dreams,
crumbles like stale bread
falling to my feet,
I starve.

When what was reality
sharp and clearer
than the mother's love for her child
abruptly disappears in a chilling mist
and becomes but a foggy
misleaidng and misinterpreted dream,
I become bewildered.

As all that I hold dear and love
with my entire self
piece by piece
flies farther and faster apart
with every passing hour,
I want.

When the one thing in the world,
the one
in which I could never imagine

would possibly, for any reason whatsoever,
let me down
does,
I am condemned.

When my heart
is stretched
to the moon and back
more times than I can count
making it too weak to stand on its own,

as the heat of the day
torments my body
less than the pain
does my heart and mind

as every plan I ever made,
all at once
becomes obsolete and over,

I'm Lost,

    Lost in a forest with no end:
    strange sounds,
    sharp shadows
    and echoes of what was
    and could still be.

    Lost,
    Walking endlessly,
    searching for some meaning
    where there is none.
    Questions hurt and hollow deep
    when there are no answers

        to feed the grieving hunger inside.

But still,
through all the rough and dark
rain worn trees of what was,
over every dead crackling leaf fallen,
as I walk
and trudge my way
to nowhere
while dying slowly inside,
I, in spite of everything,
want to find my way back.

When the sun refuses to rise
and light has turned
to a viscous jagged darkness
scratching at me as I try
to make my way,
I grow blind,
but still I go on.

Regrets

To the earth water falls.
Through the air water floats.
On the ground water sits.
Over land water slopes.

In the sky fire flies.
Through the night fire blazes.
All it touches fire eats.
At all who stare fire gazes.

Through the trees air blows.
On the sea air waves.
In the dessert air stirs.
In our breath air saves.

In our hands earth crumbles.
All we need earth grows.
In the mountains earth rises.
All we need earth shows.

All the water we foul.
All the fire we forget.
All the air we pollute.
All the earth we regret.

The death of an Artist

A thick choking cloud
   condemns my every breath
   into a wet cough
   that shrieks through my ears
   like a starving child
   that weeps for nourishment.

The blood in my veins
   has turned to dust
   colder than the empty soil
   Neil Armstrong placed his footprint in
   on that glorious day
   for all mankind.

My slowing pulse
   grows slighter
   as each passing truth
   gets burned into lie
   right before
   my new camera lens eyes.

I only see what is before me now;
   I can't see past my eyes anymore.
   Red is now red,
   not the glowing heat
   of ancient days.
   Blue is now just blue
   not the flowing life
   of a perfect wave of energy
   on a timeless sea.

Ended now, the story closes passively;
   paint a picture and,

you get what you see
not what you could be.

While Writing a Poem in America

Jagged thoughts spit
through my brain as-
a crocked nail gets
slammed through my skull
head first from
the inside out.

Ragged visions pour
over me
like liquid angels
flowing down my body
to spill on an empty
street.

Whispering devils fill
my soul with an awkward
unwritten secret as
filthy as a fallen man
Praying to no god.

Forgotten ideals smash
my heart while hopeful wishes
glide through my torn veins
like mud through a sprinkler.

Entangled strands smother
my mixed up mind
while the last
little sticky breath of truth
exits my mouth
as would a tiny piece of sleep
stuck in the eye.

My mangled realities float

away while a ruptured truth,
like billowy thoughts drifting to an
unknown heaven, inhales me.

Previously Published by Dogma Publications
London, England

Capital Storm

Green drops of rain
fall from the clouds
to crack our windshields,
while they grow and plunge
faster and faster
only to smack our children down.

All the while, that windy profit
squalls in from the west
to shatter our homes,
and end a way
of life that was born
simply to perish?
Would we go on
if it were not
profitable?

We have no wealth
within these things
that rip up our lives,
that swoop down from
a sky that is ill
with a fiscal scourge.
We must regain
Independence;
not spend, not lend;
end.

We Are Inhibiting Ourselves

While helpless pebbles on the shore
get tossed around
in the surf like anxious followers
of an awkward religion,
the seashells melt
from the corrosive salts
and the sultry sun
like truths that wear through the weather
of a false profits words.
    The current is strong
        in this sea where lives are awful and long.
        While filled with both love and hate,
        we choose to kill when we should create.

While powerless leaves get blown around
the almost vacant timberlands
like frightened guests
of a tenacious tyrant
with a sacrificial quota,
the beautiful new blossoms
are trampled under the feet
of an unforgiving society of currents
like subjects of a despondent government.
    These winds blast hard
        and nature can easily discard
        ideals that come from fake idols
        growing from universal departures and arrivals.

While those defenseless
furry little animals
get forced from their fruitful homes
by yellow proficient monsters
like caring philosophers from a greedy church,

those crucial, extraordinary yellow-green cures
get ignited by plutocratic societies
like great thinkers burned at the stake.
    This world is ignorant,
    yet it could be intelligent.
    We humans destroy
    those things we should employ.

Fear of Freedom

From the sky
shot the voice of deceit,
ripping the very fabric of a country
woven together
by the many
hopeful voices of freedom.
those who flew with him
believed his word
and absorbed his law as would an
infant child's mind
dipped in the decaying
dogma of a dictator
determined to die.

They were lead
away from truth.
They fell prey
to that same tyrannical curtain
that once covered all eyes
from that stage
where freedom's players play.

Deceit disguises
all difference and impression,
masking the very face
of liberty.
Yet, hers
are the eyes
that see to the very
soul of that
freeform
idea which
buries itself deep inside the hearts
of every child, woman, and man

at the time of creation.
That idea
when released
runs wild in the imaginations
of the liberated mind,
where in all space and time
one can freely resolve to leave or take
what he or she will
for another day.

Well, that day is here.
The cry that once screamed so
loudly in the many faces of tyranny:
"I am free,
free to think,
free to speak,
free to breathe and read;
I am here, and
I am free."
That cry is echoing off every
fallen man, woman, and child
wanting
to land on the waiting ears of America.
Today we must once again
declare ourselves independent
and freely resolve to
finish our fight for everyone.

For if we don't,
then deceit will win.
His way will become ours and
that will be the only way.
Law will be truth,
and truth will be dictated
by the very mind
that will forever be afraid,

afraid to change,

afraid of freedom.

God

God's Breath

Where does that cool
and almost scraping breeze go to
when it's done passing through you,
thrilling and chilling you down to the bone?
Does it propel some part of self
off to an unknown place,
somewhere warm and calm
where the palm oil stretches the nose
and the taste of the salt in the air intoxicates you,
slowly waning the senses?

Or does it steal some of your self, transport it
to the far off reaches of that crisp cold wilderness
where the white from the reflections
of that frigid frost from the sky
almost blinds you
with a blindness
in which you are finally allowed to see
for the first time
those sights that are chronically hidden
from the empirical world.

What is it in the wind
that takes you away?
Is it the God
that we all so desperately search for
yet can never quite grasp
or fully wrap our mind's fingers around?
Yes. For this God cannot be seen
or touched with the worldly sensations
that we have so wrongly
taken as our own: rock, stock, and barrel.

We must let this wind

scrape away these illusions
that delude us
into alluding our selves.
The alternative is a build up of lies,
a masque, a weakening of the soul,
one that so often happens
in this religio-empirical world
that puts up fences to keep the very wind out
that is here to save us
all.

God's Snakes

Our lives
are like
those of snakes.
We watch them
shed their skins
and think nothing
of it.
God watches us
shed our
skins.
We are
snakes
to God.

Sweet & Sour

When the soft crisp comfort of the cold
   washes over you in the creation of the night
   like a cool gentle mist
   on a sultry summer day might,
      Listen and then mind.
While the cricket clamoring bustle
   crackles beneath the silent blanket of the earth
   singing to the all who'll listen
   to their inborn melodies of birth,
      hear and you'll find

      your place in it all, a space
      where only you fit
      like the last grey stone
      to perfectly finish a much needed wall
      that completes a house that holds
      the only home you know.

When darkness buries the light
   just leaving those tiny specks of fire behind
   for all to know and see their way
   burning cool but bright in time,
      Look and then learn.
While the night wind blows
   slowly lifting the sails of every tree
   on the vast ocean of earth
   flawlessly spinning for all to see,
      observe and you'll yearn

      to feel it all at the same time:
      every bubbling drop of water
      on every bouncing brook,
      every sad and happy tear
      in every sweet and sour book.

When the sun ascends to pierce the night
   like a red balloon lost at a county fair
   pushing itself higher and farther
   than even the keenest eye can stare,
       Look and love.
While our glowing bronze ball rolls over head
   bouncing around our home,
   and every single speck of energy rises to meet the day
   making every single journey a life of its own,
       Listen to and love

       the world which you were given.
       It remains your only way of witnessing the life
       in every patch of grass, every drop of rain,
       every child's laugh and every ounce of pain.

Middle Ground

Two meaningless points
in time
growing further apart,
these dots
are the days
that we perceive to be
our lives.
Yet, it is with
what we fill in that blank
that makes us.

Our slice of space,
which is at the center
of our existence,
is the core
of our eternity.
That place,
not the apparent
beginning or end,
is life.

But, when we are torn
from the middle
by the beginning
and at the same time
ripped away
by the end,
we're found wanting.

If we persist,
dwelling on these points,
we produce a barren pit deep within us
filled only with the emptiness of a pain

that numbs us to the true heartbeat of life.
However,
if we live in the center,
focused on what and not when we are,
we have grown our own
paradise.

Therefore, we must surround ourselves
with centers,
not those who long
to separate from them,
and together
construct cathedrals
in the mind, the core
of our apple.

Heaven is hell,
Light is darkness,
and
life is death. The middle
is where it's all viable,
the only place.
So, we must produce
this middle space
and make it
our home.

In the name of Knowledge

From the east I feel
  the fire of a rising stench
  of evil discontent.
Yet, to the west I look
  and wait to see a glimmer
  of a wish for the joy of knowing.
Still beneath me pours the cries
  of those who know not
  what they do
       In the name of Knowledge.

Off my right hand spills
  the love of a people wronged
  by fate,
And from my left ,
  droplets of woe stain the ground
  walked upon by a dying race.
And finally at my feet,
  the wicked pain of ignorance
  is driven from my soul
  to purify me
       In the name of Knowledge.

History

A Night with Bruno (Giordano)
Venice 1591

From within the thick and wet darkness
soon grew a glowing glassy light
on the black and watery horizon.
Time seemed to stand still,
although with the ever fastening
tick tock of the waves under the ship,
we rose and fell again with the orange radiance of
what I thought was the city
flickering with a thousand tiny fire flies
fighting for some space
as if in a tall whippy pine tree back home.

But as the shore crept upon our ship,
the lights scattered into distinct ranks.
As if suddenly afraid, the small lightening bugs fled.
I could see the hundreds of torches aglow,
from the smallest candles
waving from windows lining the streets,
to the burning fires loose in the main lane;
they danced around in the night air like
burning angels waiting for something assured.

The city was alive and buzzing
with a peculiar excitement I couldn't
quite wrap my mind around.
Everyone on the ship was itching feverishly
with the hungry anticipation of finally going ashore.
We had bounced along at sea for quite a spell
and the colorful carnival frenzy of what we watched
in Florence on that evening was a welcomed change
to the salty boredom of a blank blue slate
and rough worn plank walks day upon rolling day.

There were cheers and songs sung
all over the deck and from below
as we grew ever nearer
to the approaching port.
"Land, women, and wine, hooray,"
a drunken old fat and worn man next to me exhaled.

I myself was looking forward
to a little excitement in fair Florence
and could not wait to meet the man
who proclaimed that everyone has the right
and obligation to look at the world
through his own eyes
at what lies beyond.

As I waited to hit the pier,
I could roughly hear the drones of crowds'
humming in the streets
growing louder and sharper until
the vocal roar of citizens cramming together
burst toward the sky.
"There must be a great holiday and celebration tonight,"
I thought to myself.
People seemed to be running
in every direction, and there was an uneasy awe
that hung heavy and low in the air.
The fog filled air softly crept
along with a strange odor
of some food foreign to me.
I didn't care;
I was anxious and hungry.
I could hear others on the ship
talking of the strange and wondrous smells.
Most mouths were watering,
looking forward to something to eat
besides old oranges and stale bread.

"Take a line,"
rang out one of the deck hands;
and before I knew it,
the gang plank fell and the ship emptied.
I spilled out upon the dock
with majority of the other eager aliens
weary from the hard wet voyage.
And as I bumped and shoved my way
to the end of the pier, I decided to wait
there by the bow of the ship
and avoid the often quick wet trip
overboard into the dark unknown
waters of Florence.

As the crowd began to thin out,
I made my way ashore.
I stared up a long cobblestone walkway
that ran parallel to the beach and met a tiny road.
I could hear what I thought was a grand celebration,
The loud frenzy of, food, talk, and drink.
I followed the buzz
and headed towards all the excitement and fervor
coming from somewhere that seemed close.
I couldn't see the party yet,
but still I could smell the feast
and hear the screams of excitement in a foreign tongue
tearing through my ears.

But as I drew nearer, I saw more of a main street
centrally located in the city.
The sounds began to change;
they took a new, strange and awful shape in my ears.
The screams that I thought
were expressions of joy
sounded more like horrible cries of pain.

Shrieks and sorrowful moans
unlike any I had ever heard
swarmed from a crowd around the towering
bonfires just in front of me.
I only caught glimpses of the obvious spectacle
playing within the fire's gaze
from between shoulders,
around necks, and through the legs of the
attentive audience.
Then,

    "My God!"

To my horror and absolute unbelieving eye,
I saw the most terrible site
I have to this day ever witnessed.
I stood buckled under in awful truth before my eyes.
Never had I witnessed such utter evil and waste.
Those screams were not of drinking joy
or jubilant fun from dancing in the streets;
they came from mothers, sisters, daughters,
fathers, brothers and sons. They were held,
pulled back, torn away from the fires
by some guards of what
seemed to be of the church.
And as I grew nearer, what thought I'd seen,
and what that smell turned out to be
were six human beings, hands bound
and tied screaming to stakes.
They were being burned .

    "My God," I screamed again.
"What is this, and why?"
As I stood, I stared amazed,
almost glued to the terrible site
like the rest, why I don't know.

Finally, I turned my head away
to shield my mind from such thoughts and sights,
but to my further terror,
I saw a woman lost on her knees.
She was wailing, reaching toward the flames
and the scorched torture of what
I knew was a loved one.
In her eyes was a pain ringing
louder than the busy crowd,
a pain that I felt instantly
shooting through my body
rocking my very core.
It was a suffering too ignored in this
stranded corner of the world.
Anyone not failing or immune to conscience
could feel the tangibility of the
splintered agony I saw in her eyes.
The tears poured from both eyes
like white water on a mountain,
a river that was just not strong enough
to extinguish the pain of the fire
which consumed these people.

Lost & Found

A smile more brilliant than
the morning sun
just peeking through the yellow curtains
always began my day
with the bright and happy world
that was you.

Rolling over in paradise,
brushing your soft leg with mine,
gently grazing your sweet glowing cheek
with the back tips of my fingers,
you were there,
and our kiss perpetually joined us together
every day.

A laugh,
that came with a tickle
or a word, or even a funny smile
rang the harmony of home
full in my ears
every time I heard yours.

A hug, tighter
than an empty and hollow
make believe embrace
surrounded me with a love
that I'd searched for forever
and had finally found
lying deep within your arms.

Where will it go,
this lost and found love

that only comes once
in an existence?

Will it fade like an old memory,
first by an hour, then by day, and week, and month, and year
until it's hard to be convinced that it ever existed,
a picture of a dream in a cloud
high in the air
blown away by a dark and cold wind?

Jerome White was born and raised in Virginia. He writes poetry, fiction, non-fiction, and music. He also paints, creates graphic art and designs websites. He most recently published L'Angelica: History Through the Eyes of Angels, also available from Dominion House. He received both his undergraduate and graduate degrees from Old Dominion University in Virginia where he also began his teaching career. He is now the Department Head for Arts & Sciences at ECPI College of Technology

Check out more of his work at:
http://gerrywhite.com

www.ingramcontent.com/pod-product-compliance
Lightning Source LLC
Chambersburg PA
CBHW031650040426
42453CB00006B/257